The Basis of Christian Support for Israel

Rev. Malcolm Hedding

Biblical Zionism Series – Part I

The Basis of Christian Support for Israel
Rev. Malcolm Hedding

ISBN: 978-0-9765297-0-5

Copyright©2004 by:
International Christian Embassy Jerusalem – USA, Inc.
PO Box 332974, Murfreesboro, TN 37133

The International Christian Embassy Jerusalem was founded in 1980 as an act of comfort and solidarity with Israel and the Jewish people in their claim to Jerusalem.

From our headquarters in Jerusalem and through our branches and representatives in over 80 nations, we seek to challenge the church to take up its scriptural responsibilities towards the Jewish people, to remind Israel of the wonderful promises made to her in the Bible, and to be a source of practical assistance to all the people of the land of Israel.

All scriptures are taken from *The New King James Version*. 1996, c1982. Thomas Nelson: Nashville

All rights reserved. No part of this book may be used or reproduced in any form without written permission from the author, except in the case of brief quotations in reviews or critical articles.

CONTENTS

Vehicle of World Redemption	5
The Abrahamic Covenant	19
The Threefold Call of Israel	27
Israel's Return Home	45

Vehicle of World Redemption

Christian support for Israel, or Biblical Zionism, is not based on the prophetic portions of the Word of God. That might sound quite strange to some of you who have for years had Israel presented to you as a type of eschatology or in a prophetic context. We need to understand that the reason we support Israel is not based on the prophetic portions of God's Word.

Our support for Israel is based on something far deeper, and that is the promises of the Word of God or the great covenants of history that God made with the people of Israel. The prophetic portions of God's Word reinforce these great promises and validate them. But the basis of Christian support for Israel is not the prophetic passages; it is indeed the great covenants that God made with this nation.

Then, if we have to put God's plan with Israel into a particular context, that context is the wider eternal plan of God for the world and the nation of Israel. That is God's redemptive plan. God's redemptive plan did not begin in time. It began before time in the state of eternity.

³ Blessed *be* the God and Father of our Lord Jesus Christ, who has blessed us with every spiritual blessing in the heavenly *places* in Christ, ⁴ just as He chose us in Him before the

Basis of Christian Support for Israel

foundation of the world, that we should be holy and without blame before Him in love, [5] having predestined us to adoption as sons by Jesus Christ to Himself, according to the good pleasure of His will, [6] to the praise of the glory of His grace, by which He made us accepted in the Beloved.
[7] In Him we have redemption through His blood, the forgiveness of sins, according to the riches of His grace [8] which He made to abound toward us in all wisdom and prudence, [9] having made known to us the mystery of His will, according to His good pleasure which He purposed in Himself, [10] that in the dispensation of the fullness of the times He might gather together in one all things in Christ, both which are in heaven and which are on earth—in Him.
[11] In Him also we have obtained an inheritance, being predestined according to the purpose of Him who works all things according to the counsel of His will, [12] that we who first trusted in Christ should be to the praise of His glory.
[13] In Him you also *trusted,* after you heard the word of truth, the gospel of your salvation; in whom also, having believed, you were sealed with the Holy Spirit of promise, [14] who is the guarantee of our inheritance until the redemption of the purchased possession, to the praise of His glory.   *(Ephesians 1:3-14)*

Verse 4 says: "Just as He chose us in Him before the foundation of the world." Before God made anything - before He laid the foundations of this wonderful earth upon which we dwell - the divine plan was initiated. It was in the eternal state that the only one true God, who subsequently revealed Himself in the Word of God, undertook to create man and redeem him through the death of His Son.

Though Israel became the vehicle of this redemptive plan, the goal was the world. It is important for us to know that.

The Story of God's Love for the World

The story of Israel is the story of God's love for the world. He is not a God given to respecting persons. God has no favorites. In the second chapter of Romans the Apostle Paul tells us that there are a number of principles that God employs when He judges the human race.

He judges without respect of persons. Therefore, He treats all people the same regardless of who they are - whether they be Jews or Gentiles.

> [11] For there is no partiality with God.
> [12] For as many as have sinned without law will also perish without law, and as many as have sinned in the law will be judged by the law.
> *(Romans 2:11-12)*

How wonderful is that scripture in John 3:16 that we all know and love where God declares His love for all mankind!

> [3] For God so loved the world that He gave His only begotten Son that whosoever believes in Him should not perish but have everlasting life.
> *(John 3:16)*

So the story of Israel is not a story of a people that God loves more than another. It is important for us to know that. To be sure, it is a unique story, but it is one that has to do with the way in which this holy, loving God reaches the world with His message in the Messiah.

Israel is the vehicle of world redemption; therefore, to curse her or hate her or despise her is to resist the purpose of God - eternal salvation - flowing to the world through her.

In the beginning of the great book of Romans the Apostle Paul is speaking of God's world agenda. He is painting with a very broad brush. He speaks of the glory of God that is to be seen in creation. He talks to us about how God reveals Himself in the natural order. Having gone through this wonderful discourse about the glory of God and human responsibility toward Him, Paul then recognizes that his readers must be asking a question.

The question that his readers are asking is, "Okay, Paul, you are talking about a God who engages the world. You are talking about a God who can be seen and understood in that which He has created. You are talking about an incredible God who made everything, and therefore all of humanity is accountable to Him. So where do the Jewish people fit in? For what reason do they exist?"

In Romans 3:1-2 he rhetorically asks the question, "What advantage then has the Jew?" That is the question in their minds and he answers the question, "Much in every way because to them were committed the oracles of God."

So herein lies the chief reason why the nation of Israel came into existence. They came into existence to be the custodians of world redemption, the vehicle by which God would bring His message of eternal salvation to the world.

For that reason, to curse this nation or to despise this nation or to hate this nation is to resist the plan of God for the world.

Israel's Unique Role

Her position before God is special because she plays out a role historically that is unique to her. No other nation has this role. This role has been misunderstood and time and time again it has been challenged by the powers of darkness, but it will never fail.

The role that God has given to the Jewish people He has bound up with the redemption of the world. If the nation of Israel fails, then God's plan for world redemption fails. She is the vehicle of world redemption.

The God of history then, and of the Bible, has guaranteed her survival. She is the apple of His eye.

[8] For thus says the LORD of hosts: "He sent Me after glory, to the nations which plunder you; for he who touches you touches the apple of His eye." *(Zechariah 2:8)*

What does this mean? Does this mean that Israel is more loved than other nations? Some Christians think so, or if they do not think so they behave as if they think so.

But what does this mean when God says, "Be careful what you do with these people"? "Do not touch them, do not hate them, do not curse them because they are the apple of my eye"? What does that mean? It simply means that He affords her special care but does not love her more than another people.

Just like a pregnant woman is afforded special care by her family members, they look after her a bit more. They care for her, they open the door for her, and they make sure she is comfortable, because she has a peculiar role to play out within the family context. Nevertheless, all the family members are loved exactly the same and that is the truth of God's Word when it comes to the nation of Israel.

She is the apple of His eye but she is not loved more than other people. She lives out and plays out a peculiar role in history, and therefore she has to be cared for.

Her uniqueness lies in the fact that she is the custodian of the Word of God. It can be said, therefore, that the nation of Israel exists for the Messiah. That is absolutely true.

The Coming of Messiah

Why did Israel come into existence? Israel came into existence for one reason: for the Messiah. She prepared the world for His coming, she brought Him into the world, and she will bring Him back at the consummation of the age. He did not come in a

Basis of Christian Support for Israel

vacuum. He came in a context so that He could stand up in Jerusalem and say, "As Isaiah said," and "As David said." He had, therefore, messianic credentials. He did not come in a vacuum.

Israel provided the context for His arrival. She birthed Him into the world and He will come back again because of the nation of Israel. She, like all the peoples of the world, needs Him, and is fallen and totally depraved. She is no different.

Sin has destroyed the image of God in humankind, meaning that, whether we be Jew or Gentile, we have no understanding of God. We have no desire to seek God and our wisdom is nothing but foolishness.

The Apostle Paul in Romans 8:7 says that the natural man does not seek God, neither can he, because he is carnally minded. It also says that we are enemies of God because of this thing called sin. We are therefore unable to find our way home or even understand or seek for the God of the Bible. Jew and Gentile are in exactly the same position. Jesus is the only answer.

All of history is summed up in Him and even the universe is summed up in Him and has meaning in His person. This is why we read in the beginning of the book of Ephesians that all of creation is summed up in the person of Jesus. All things find their meaning in the Messiah and His work - His finished work on the cross - is the only way in which perfected men and women can be created.

His finished work on the cross is the only way in which the plan of God from all eternity can be accomplished. He died on that cross, once for all to create perfect men and women who reflect the image of God and who will fellowship with and serve Him for all eternity.

This is why the book of Ephesians declares again in chapter 1 that when we are redeemed by the grace of God, we will live for the praise of His glory. What a wonderful thing! The Westminster Confession, of course, says that the chief end of man is to glorify God and to enjoy Him forever.

I do not serve God just to be obedient or because this is what I have to do to keep my eternal insurance intact. No, we live to be to the praise of His glory and we enjoy the God that we love and serve. So, if we look at this incredible redemptive plan that was brought forth before the foundation of the world, we realize that Jesus died theologically before time.

Revelation 13:8 says, "He died before the foundation of the world." Paul says that we were chosen in Him before the world began. That means there was a decision before time that He would die. It is wonderful!

Jesus died theologically before time but He died actually in time around A.D. 30. This means that He gave His word to His Father before time began that He would assume a human body and die for a world that would fall if created.

Fascinating! So, when Adam and Eve sinned in the garden, God did not decide to go to Plan B because Plan A failed. God knew beforehand that if He wanted to create humankind with the ability to choose, they would be perfectly inquisitive. So, if there was something beyond what God said, man would think about it and fall. He would not believe that what God says is true. He would rebel against God; but, Jesus died before the world began. That is, God made provision for our sin and rebellion before He made us.

Paul understood this and so in the Second book of Timothy he writes:

[9] who has saved us and called *us* with a holy calling, not according to our works, but according to His own purpose and grace which was given to us in Christ Jesus before time began. *(II Timothy 1:9)*

This purpose began before time but He came in time, assumed a human body and died on the cross for us all so that we can all be to the praise of the glory of His grace.

Why Israel?

Israel brought it all home to earth as the conduit or delivery vehicle of world redemption. God needed Israel to be the vehicle by which He would bring this redemptive purpose into the world. God did not choose Israel because she was strong, capable, wise, or anything of that nature.

The Word of God says that He chose Israel because He chose her - not because of anything that was in her. He chose her because He loved her and that was it - not because of her ability or her strength.

If you turn to the book of Deuteronomy, you find this clearly stated in chapter 7:

> [6] "For you *are* a holy people to the LORD your God; the LORD your God has chosen you to be a people for Himself, a special treasure above all the peoples on the face of the earth. [7] The LORD did not set His love on you nor choose you because you were more in number than any other people, for you were the least of all peoples; [8] but because the LORD loves you, and because He would keep the oath which He swore to your fathers, the LORD has brought you out with a mighty hand, and redeemed you from the house of bondage, from the hand of Pharaoh king of Egypt." *(Deuteronomy 7:6-8)*

This story is about the choice of a nation and a promise that God makes to this nation's fathers. He chose Israel simply because He chose her. He will completely fulfill His redemptive plan, and He alone will get the glory. In spite of her weaknesses, in spite of her failings, in spite of all of history, God will fulfill His plan through Israel and in the end He will get the glory.

That is why in Romans 11, the Apostle Paul, having talked at length about the plan of God and the nation of Israel, ends that chapter in a eulogy. He is overcome with a sense of the sovereignty of God. He recognizes that even though Israel is weak, has rejected the messianic credentials of the Messiah and has rebelled against God historically - in spite of all this, God has fulfilled His plan through her. Indeed, He used much of her rebellion and even unbelief in order to further His plan.

So he concludes that great and marvelous chapter with:

> [33] Oh, the depth of the riches both of the wisdom and knowledge of God! How unsearchable are His judgments and His ways past finding out!
> [34] *"For who has known the mind of the LORD? Or who has become His counselor?"*
> [35] *"Or who has first given to Him And it shall be repaid to him?"*
> [36] For of Him and through Him and to Him are all things, to whom be glory forever. Amen.
> *(Romans 11:33-36)*

God will fulfill His plan through Israel!

The story of Israel is the story of the Messiah. She will yet come to understand this but as we shall see, even her rejection of His messianic credentials has furthered the eternal plan of God for world redemption.

This, then, is the context in which we are to understand the basis of Christian support of Israel. It is important for us to know this. This is the backdrop in front of which the drama of world redemption is played out on the stage of human history. It is an eternal backdrop. It is a backdrop of God's purpose that took root before the foundation of the world.

The main player in this incredible story of world redemption is in fact Israel. Not because she is favored but because her role secures a vast family from every nation and every tribe of the earth for the God of heaven.

We would then expect the Jewish people to occupy the center stage of world history, and they do. There is not a week that goes by, I am sure you have noticed, without Israel being in the news.

Israel is a tiny nation, five to six million people in a very, very small land. But she occupies the center stage of world history. This is because she enjoys this peculiar role of taking that which was birthed before time and bringing it to earth in time so that God can redeem for Himself men and women from every tribe and from every tongue in the world. It is incredible. It is amazing, that this is the back drop.

The Mystery of Israel

[25] Now to Him who is able to establish you according to my gospel and the preaching of Jesus Christ, according to the revelation of the mystery kept secret since the world began [26] but now made manifest, and by the prophetic Scriptures made known to all nations, according to the commandment of the everlasting God, for obedience to the faith— [27] to God, alone wise, *be* glory through Jesus Christ forever. Amen.
(Romans 16:25-27)

This is a fascinating little portion of the Word of God. It tells us the definition of a biblical mystery. I have no doubt that in the context of Romans 16, the Apostle Paul is speaking about the mystery of the church. But while he is doing that, he gives us the principle of a biblical mystery.

Basis of Christian Support for Israel

The Apostle Paul did not discover something that no one else had discovered. It wasn't as if he had a revelation that was brand new and was never written anywhere. That is not what he is saying. He actually is saying that a biblical mystery was always in the pages of scripture. At the right time, in the purpose of God, the Holy Spirit shone upon the Apostle Paul's mind and upon the minds of the other apostles and revealed to them the truth of the pages of God's Word.

The Bible says that there are many mysteries, not just one. There is the mystery of the church, and there is the mystery of the resurrection. We understand that the resurrection is a mystery. How will God infuse us with the power that will make our aging, frail bodies eternal, firm, and incredible – is this not beyond our ability to understand?

I remember years ago I had a remarkable dream of the second coming of Jesus. I will never forget it, because in the dream I could literally feel my body changing as it rushed toward heaven to meet Jesus in the sky. The experience was so real that it impacted me for months. In the dream, I could feel the incredible power of God surging through every part of my body. I could feel the insides of my body changing. It was really wonderful. Sad it was only a dream. But it will happen one day! That is the mystery of the resurrection.

Then there is the mystery of the second coming that Paul speaks about, and there is also the mystery of Israel.

[25] For I do not desire, brethren, that you should be ignorant of this mystery, lest you should be wise in your own opinion, that blindness in part has happened to Israel until the fullness of the Gentiles has come in. *(Romans 11:25)*

So, understanding Israel has always been difficult for the church because it is a mystery.

The Abrahamic Covenant

Abraham encountered God and God said that what He was about to do through him and the nation that would come from him would indeed impact the whole world. Abraham would inherit the world. So who was this man, Abram? After God ratified the covenant with him, God renamed him Abraham.

The Man Abraham

The book of Romans also tells us that he was a Gentile. He was living in Ur of the Chaldeans. According to the Talmud (ancient rabbinic writings) we have come to believe that he came from a family of idol manufacturers. Something incredible must have happened to this man, because he encountered the one true God.

I can just see him. He comes home from his long day at work and he walks into the kitchen where his wife Sarah greets him by saying, "How were things today, Lovey?"

He says, "Great. Guess what? God spoke to me."

And then she must have said, "Which one? The one out of wood that you are about to finish or is it the other one out of stone?"

"No," he says. "Actually, God spoke to me."

By this time she is getting a little nervous because she says, "What did He say?" He says, "We are leaving."

She says, "And where are we going?" He says, "I have no idea."

The Bible says he went out not knowing where he was going but he was looking for a city which has foundations and whose architect and builder is God. How many women would follow their husband if they came home and told them a story like that?

Especially if he was fairly wealthy and had a lot of security – suddenly your husband appears to lose his marbles. "We are going where?" "I do not know." "How?" "I will follow this God."

It is a remarkable story. It tells us, dear friends, that the encounter that this man had with God was little short of amazing; it was absolutely overwhelming.

It must have been so overwhelming that he could not doubt it at all. He did not have a DVD or a Bible or a video machine or a Christian book. He had nothing that we have to use as milestones on his pilgrimage. He did not have a congregation and he did not have a pastor that he could go to.

But he had such an encounter with God that the great program of world redemption rested on his decision. Is that not astonishing? Subsequently, he went out to follow this God and left everything.

Hebrews 11 talks about this incredible meeting that God had with Abraham.

> [8] By faith Abraham obeyed when he was called to go out to the place which he would receive as an inheritance. And he went out, not knowing where he was going. [9] By faith he dwelt in the land of promise as *in* a foreign country, dwelling in tents with Isaac and Jacob, the heirs with him of the same promise; [10] for he waited for the city which has foundations, whose builder and maker *is* God. *(Hebrews 11:8-10)*

So the fascinating thing in this story about Abraham is the following. It is probably true that when God met with him He showed him the end game. He showed him that heavenly city to which we are all moving that exists in eternity.

It is therefore proof that this thing began in eternity and will end in eternity. What he saw was so incredible. He saw a city that was like none other. It had foundations that never moved. There was nothing in the universe, not even a nuclear bomb, that could rock this city. It had foundations. When he looked at its beauty and the God who made it, his mind was made up. He would follow this God into eternity.

The beauty of that city so overwhelmed him that he gave up everything so as to build a road home toward it for every man, woman and child. It can be said that Abraham is the great road builder of all eternity. He would find a way in the purpose of God to bring us all home.

That is why God said to him, as recorded in Romans 4, that he would inherit the world. That is, he would be the natural father of all the redeemed.

> [13] For the promise that he would be the heir of the world *was* not to Abraham or to his seed through the law, but through the righteousness of faith. *(Romans 4:13)*

So when you get to heaven one day, please do not look for Peter. Now we love Peter, do we not? Peter had a motto. Do you know what his motto in life was? "When in doubt, speak out." He lived by that code. Time and time again he put his foot in his mouth! We love him and we do not diminish his status, but how many of you have heard the story that when you get to heaven, Peter will be at the gate? Tell your friends he will not be!

Abraham will be at the gate because he is the father of us all. God said he would inherit the world and that is why his name, Abraham, means the father of many nations. So we read about this in Genesis 12.

> [1] Now the LORD had said to Abram:
> "Get out of your country,
> From your family
> And from your father's house,
> To a land that I will show you.
> [2] I will make you a great nation;
> I will bless you
> And make your name great;
> And you shall be a blessing.
> [3] I will bless those who bless you,
> And I will curse him who curses you;

And in you all the families of the earth shall be blessed." *(Genesis 12:1-3)*

It is interesting to see that when God encountered Abraham and sent him out, He gave him a threefold call that would play itself out as time passed. So here we have this Gentile who is encountered by God in such an incredible way that he sees eternity. He goes out to follow God. This, dear friends, gives us a definition of a Jew. It is very important.

Who or what is a Jew? A Jew is a Gentile who has been brought into a peculiar relationship with God for the purpose of world redemption.

That definition is important because of anti-Semitism. Anti-Semitism often suggests that Jewish people do not belong to this planet or to the human race – they are so different that they do not belong here. The fact is that the Word of God teaches that this man was just a Gentile who was brought into this peculiar relationship with God in order to bring millions of men and women home to the city of God. That is who he is.

That is why in Romans 4 the Apostle Paul is making this point: that Abraham is the father of the Gentiles. Why? Because God called him when he was a Gentile. He is also the father of the Jews because he was later circumcised.

> [11] And he received the sign of circumcision, a seal of the righteousness of the faith which *he had while still* uncircumcised, that he might be the father of all those who believe, though they are uncircumcised, that righteousness might be imputed to them also, [12] and the father of

circumcision to those who not only *are* of the circumcision, but who also walk in the steps of the faith which our father Abraham *had while still* uncircumcised. *(Romans 4:11-12)*

He shows the Gentiles the way of salvation which is, simply put, faith in God. He also shows the Jewish world the way of salvation, which is faith in God.

[12] and the father of circumcision to those who not only *are* of the circumcision, but who also walk in the steps of the faith which our father Abraham *had while still* uncircumcised.
(Romans 4:12)

Who is Abraham? He is a Jew. Who is Abraham? He is a Gentile. First and foremost he was a Gentile brought into this peculiar relationship with God for the sake of world redemption. So he will be the natural foundation upon which God's redemptive plan in time will be built and in the end, this will bring millions of men, women, and children from all over the world home.

The Covenant

God's call to Abraham took the form of a covenant. This covenant is called the Abrahamic covenant and it is mentioned on numerous occasions from Genesis 13 onwards. Genesis 17 is another part of the story where God again reminds Abraham of His covenant with him.

[7] "And I will establish My covenant between Me and you and your descendants after you in their generations, for an everlasting covenant, to be God to you and your descendants after you.

⁸ Also I give to you and your descendants after you the land in which you are a stranger, all the land of Canaan, as an everlasting possession; and I will be their God." *(Genesis 17:7-8)*

It is interesting to note in the book of Galatians that the Apostle Paul says if you belong to Jesus, then you are Abraham's children according to this covenant.

²⁹ And if you *are* Christ's, then you are Abraham's seed, and heirs according to the promise. *(Galatians 3:29)*

There are many today who tell us that God has no national destiny for the Jewish people - that He has withdrawn the Abrahamic covenant from the Jewish people because of their disobedience. If that be true then we cannot be Abraham's children according to the promise of God. If that be true, then what Paul says here in Galatians 3:29 is just nonsense.

The fact of the matter is that God has not withdrawn his Abrahamic covenant from the Jewish people. The truth is, the Abrahamic covenant and God's call over the man Abraham had a lot to do with the world and eternity and not just with the Jewish people.

Abraham saw a city in eternity. It was that city that inspired him to leave Ur and follow God. So the Abrahamic covenant is more than just a covenant with the Jewish people. It is God's promise, God's initiative to save the world,. For that reason, if you belong to Jesus, then you are Abraham's children according to the promise.

That is why the Abrahamic covenant is so important. When the Word of God uses the word everlasting, as it does in Genesis 17, it really means everlasting.

The Abrahamic covenant first of all is a bequest because it bequeaths to the Jewish people the land of Canaan as an everlasting possession.

It secondly has a threefold call which we will examine in the next chapter.

And thirdly, it constitutes a warning. We have touched on the warning in the previous chapter. The warning is that if you curse these people you are meddling in God's purpose for world redemption, and therefore you set yourself against His purpose and He will curse you.

However, if you bless them and if you help them and stand alongside them, then God will bless you because you are standing alongside the vehicle of world redemption. You are working with His purpose for the blessing of the world so that millions of men, women, and children can go to the city. Hallelujah!

That is why standing with Israel even until today is important for church growth. If you want the blessing of God upon your church, then stand with Israel.

The Threefold Call of Israel

God came to Abraham and gave him a threefold call. I want to spend a little time in this section examining the threefold call given to Abraham. This call in its threefold character is understood when we examine the different times when God came to Abraham to announce and reestablish the covenant with him.

The Birthing Call

The first call or role that the Jewish people play out in history is what we call a birthing call. God says in Genesis 12 that in Abraham all the families of the earth will be blessed. "I am doing something to you, Abraham, and to the nation that comes from you that will be for the blessing of every nation upon the face of the earth."

To put it another way, the nation of Israel would bring redemptive products into the world. So the story of salvation is in fact a Jewish one, in that all that we hold dear and appreciate as God's people is in fact Jewish. Paul reminds us of this in Romans 9.

> [1] I tell the truth in Christ, I am not lying, my conscience also bearing me witness in the Holy Spirit, [2] that I have great sorrow and continual grief in my heart. [3] For I could wish that I

myself were accursed from Christ for my brethren, my countrymen according to the flesh, [4] who are Israelites, to whom *pertain* the adoption, the glory, the covenants, the giving of the law, the service *of God,* and the promises; [5] of whom *are* the fathers and from whom, according to the flesh, Christ *came,* who is over all, *the* eternally blessed God. Amen.

(Romans 9:1-5)

Jesus also affirms this in the Gospel according to John in the fourth chapter where He says that "salvation is of the Jews" (John 4:22). So the things we hold dear and love as Christians are all Jewish - including this wonderful book, the Bible.

As we have discussed earlier in this book, the Apostle Paul tells us that the chief reason for which the nation of Israel came into existence was and is to be the custodians of the Word of God. The nation of Israel was chosen to serve the world.

In chapter 12 of the book of Revelation, John the Apostle has a revelation concerning the nation of Israel. He says that a sign appears of a pregnant woman clothed with the sun, the moon, and the stars.

> [1] Now a great sign appeared in heaven: a woman clothed with the sun, with the moon under her feet, and on her head a garland of twelve stars. [2] Then being with child, she cried out in labor and in pain to give birth.
>
> *(Revelation 12:1-2)*

The woman is Israel. The imagery comes from the book of Genesis.

Basis of Christian Support for Israel

⁹ Then he dreamed still another dream and told it to his brothers, and said, "Look, I have dreamed another dream. And this time, the sun, the moon, and the eleven stars bowed down to me." ¹⁰ So he told *it* to his father and his brothers; and his father rebuked him and said to him, "What *is* this dream that you have dreamed? Shall your mother and I and your brothers indeed come to bow down to the earth before you?" ¹¹ And his brothers envied him, but his father kept the matter *in mind.* *(Genesis 37:9-11)*

This is the story of our friend, Joseph, who is something of a dreamer - and his dreams infuriate everybody. In some ways we can appreciate why his brothers were annoyed with him. He was the youngest, and it must be quite disconcerting when your younger brother comes to you and says, "You know, I had a dream last night and in this dream you all came and bowed down to me."

It is quite clear, then, that what Revelation 12 is talking about is exactly the same picture. It is the nation of Israel, the twelve tribes of Israel. Moreover, the woman Israel is pregnant. Here is the birthing call: "In you all the nations of the earth will be blessed" (Genesis 12:3).

Why will the nations be blessed? Because they will be the recipients of heaven's redeeming purpose through her. Most of all, she will exist for the Messiah. If you look at Revelation 12, the story goes on and tells us that she brings a male Child into the world who is destined to rule the world with a rod of iron. Very interesting.

> [5] She bore a male Child who was to rule all nations with a rod of iron. And her Child was caught up to God and His throne.
> *(Revelation 12:5)*

She exists for the male Child and the male Child has a destiny that will one day bring Him back to earth to rule every nation with a rod of iron.

This is Israel's remarkable calling in history. The woman of Revelation 12 is not the church as some assume because the church did not bring Jesus into the world; Israel brought Jesus into the world. And Jesus brought the church into the world or into existence.

Here again we have Israel's birthing call reinforced. As a consequence we do thank God for all that we have received from the Jewish people. It is amazing that a people who are no different than any other, a people who are just as weak and sinful as any other, a people who are small and maybe smaller than most and weaker than most has given us these amazing gifts. Gifts that lead us into the knowledge of God, deliver us from sin, give us eternal life and will finally lead us into that city.

The Suffering Call

Then there is a second call that God gives to the nation of Israel, and here we turn back to the book of Genesis, chapter 15.

⁷ Then He said to him, "I *am* the LORD, who brought you out of Ur of the Chaldeans, to give you this land to inherit it."
⁸ And he said, "Lord GOD, how shall I know that I will inherit it?"
⁹ So He said to him, "Bring Me a three-year-old heifer, a three-year-old female goat, a three-year-old ram, a turtledove, and a young pigeon."
¹⁰ Then he brought all these to Him and cut them in two, down the middle, and placed each piece opposite the other; but he did not cut the birds in two. ¹¹ And when the vultures came down on the carcasses, Abram drove them away.
¹² Now when the sun was going down, a deep sleep fell upon Abram; and behold, horror *and* great darkness fell upon him. *(Genesis 15:7-12)*

Here the Abrahamic covenant is made with God. He brings the sacrificial carcasses to the place where the covenant will be cut or made and he cuts them in two. Then, suddenly, the vultures come down to attack this covenant that God is making with Abraham.

The vulture is a symbol of the evil and demonic powers of darkness. They are vicious-looking creatures, since they are large, have bald heads, long beaks and long talons, and normally flock en masse over a killing in the bush. The lion kills a buck or a giraffe or some other animal, and after the lions have eaten and the cheetah and the leopard have eaten and finally the hyena have eaten, then the vultures get their chance. They swoop down and tear the carcass to pieces. But in the frenzy, as they dismember the carcass and get what they can from it, they tear each other to pieces as well.

A fallen world afflicted with total depravity and dominated by a devilish, demonic reality can not but hate God and any entity that represents Him on the earth. You remember that the Apostle Paul, speaking about our human condition in the book of Ephesians, describes us in this way.

> [1] And you *He made alive,* who were dead in trespasses and sins, [2] in which you once walked according to the course of this world, according to the prince of the power of the air, the spirit who now works in the sons of disobedience, [3] among whom also we all once conducted ourselves in the lusts of our flesh, fulfilling the desires of the flesh and of the mind, and were by nature children of wrath, just as the others.
> *(Ephesians 2:1-3)*

That is who we were. We were dead, dominated and doomed. We were totally depraved, without any ability to love God or to seek Him, and the Bible says we hated Him. A world like that will seek to destroy any entity that represents God and His purpose.

So when God called Abraham into this peculiar role for the salvation of the world, inherent in that call was a suffering call. From that day onwards the vulture would descend upon the Jewish people seeking to eliminate them and to destroy them. The devil knew that if he frustrated the plan of God in the nation of Israel, he would bring to an end the great purpose of God in bringing millions of men and women into the city of God.

Basis of Christian Support for Israel

The Jewish people have suffered vicariously - that is, on behalf of the human race. They have suffered for you and for me because they became the vehicle of world redemption. They have paid an awful price to bring us God's Word. No other nation upon the face of the earth has had this peculiar role. So they have suffered on behalf of the world to give the world the knowledge of redemption.

The Apostle John writes in Revelation 12 not only of the peculiar birthing destiny of Israel, but also of another sign that goes hand in hand with that call, the sign of suffering. Israel's history has been one of pain, labor and conflict. She has given birth in a crucible of evil.

[1] Now a great sign appeared in heaven: a woman clothed with the sun, with the moon under her feet, and on her head a garland of twelve stars. [2] Then being with child, she cried out in labor and in pain to give birth. [3] And another sign appeared in heaven: behold, a great, fiery red dragon having seven heads and ten horns, and seven diadems on his heads. [4] His tail drew a third of the stars of heaven and threw them to the earth. And the dragon stood before the woman who was ready to give birth, to devour her Child as soon as it was born. [5] She bore a male Child who was to rule all nations with a rod of iron. And her Child was caught up to God and His throne. *(Revelation 12:1-5)*

Here the New Testament verifies the picture we have in Genesis 15 that the vulture would settle forever in front of the woman, seeking to devour her and tear her apart.

It is true, dear friends, that the Jewish people have suffered historically for their own rebellion and their own sins, and that is why we have the great prophets Isaiah, Jeremiah and Ezekiel, and of course the minor prophets.

We have to also admit, however, that the suffering of the nation of Israel has a supernatural and demonic dimension. Perhaps the most demonic expression historically of that suffering has been the assault of the Christian church upon the Jewish people. I mean, how can that be? It is absolutely astonishing that the powers of darkness have used Jesus' cloak and the devil's dagger to destroy the Jewish people. This is a great evil.

The people who were the recipients of Jewish redemptive products became the vulture and preyed on the Jewish people. I know that many would say, "but they were not real Christians." My dear friends, sadly, some of them were. Moreover, it is not up to the Jewish world to work out who are real Christians and who are not. These awful things happened in the name of Christianity.

In chapter 15 of Genesis, Abraham not only has to chase away the vultures, but the passage states that when he fell asleep he was overcome with horror. This is interesting because he is entering into the covenant with God that will eventually culminate with men and women entering the city of God. (He went out looking for a city.)

Basis of Christian Support for Israel

You would have thought, then, that when he entered into this remarkable covenant with God, he would have dreamt of the city and would have seen streets of gold, and angels and sights that were just too amazing and beautiful for words to somehow articulate. But he does not.

When he falls into a sleep or trance, the Bible says that deep horror filled his soul. So the God of history said, "Abraham, if you do this for the sake of the world, and if the people who come from you birth the written Word and the living Word, you have got to know that your nation will be plunged into a conflict against the powers of darkness such as no nation upon the face of the earth will ever have to endure."

My dear friends, the way in which we have negated the woman, the pregnant woman, is shameful. We have disinvested her, we have used clever theology to annul her, we have allowed the vulture to find a resting place in our own pulpits and congregations – it is quite overwhelming. After all, she was and is the vehicle of world redemption.

The Priestly Call

Then we come to a third role that God bequeaths to Abraham. This story, for me, is always deeply moving. God takes this man - this Gentile – and leads him down another road because He wants him to know everything about this plan. He wants Abraham to know what he is getting into. So the next time God comes to him, He tells him, I want you to take your son, your supernatural son, and I want you to lead him to Mount Moriah...and there you have to kill him.

¹ Now it came to pass after these things that God tested Abraham, and said to him, "Abraham!" And he said, "Here I am."
² Then He said, "Take now your son, your only *son* Isaac, whom you love, and go to the land of Moriah, and offer him there as a burnt offering on one of the mountains of which I shall tell you."
³ So Abraham rose early in the morning and saddled his donkey, and took two of his young men with him, and Isaac his son; and he split the wood for the burnt offering, and arose and went to the place of which God had told him. ⁴ Then on the third day Abraham lifted his eyes and saw the place afar off.
⁵ And Abraham said to his young men, "Stay here with the donkey; the lad and I will go yonder and worship, and we will come back to you."
⁶ So Abraham took the wood of the burnt offering and laid *it* on Isaac his son; and he took the fire in his hand, and a knife, and the two of them went together. ⁷ But Isaac spoke to Abraham his father and said, "My father!"
And he said, "Here I am, my son."
Then he said, "Look, the fire and the wood, but where *is* the lamb for a burnt offering?"
⁸ And Abraham said, "My son, God will provide for Himself the lamb for a burnt offering." So the two of them went together.
⁹ Then they came to the place of which God had told him. And Abraham built an altar there and placed the wood in order; and he bound Isaac his son and laid him on the altar, upon the wood.
¹⁰ And Abraham stretched out his hand and took the knife to slay his son.

¹¹ But the Angel of the LORD called to him from heaven and said, "Abraham, Abraham!" So he said, "Here I am."
¹² And He said, "Do not lay your hand on the lad, or do anything to him; for now I know that you fear God, since you have not withheld your son, your only *son,* from Me."
(Genesis 22:1-12)

It is a deeply moving picture. Here they are at the foot of Moriah and as they get there, they take the wood and they lay it on Isaac. Isaac puts the wood on his back. He climbs with his father up the hill. When they get there, Isaac is laid on the wood and the Bible says Abraham lifted the knife and killed him – NO. We know that an angel stepped in and stopped this.

However, the book of Hebrews says that Abraham's obedience was so complete that he actually received Isaac back from the dead because Isaac was dead in his heart. If it were not for the intervention of God, Isaac would have died that day by the hand of Abraham.

¹⁷ By faith Abraham, when he was tested, offered up Isaac, and he who had received the promises offered up his only begotten *son,* ¹⁸ of whom it was said, *"In Isaac your seed shall be called,"* ¹⁹ concluding that God *was* able to raise *him* up, even from the dead, from which he also received him in a figurative sense.
(Hebrews 11:17-19)

One of the most amazing things about this story is picked up in the New Covenant scriptures. When Abraham had Isaac on that altar of sacrifice, something happened to him. We can only construe that the Spirit of God came down upon him and took hold of him and transported him two thousand years into the future. When he awoke he found himself in Jerusalem in about the year 33 A.D.

As he looked he found himself at almost the same place, and when he cleared his eyes he saw the form of a skull in the hill. For Skull Hill is in fact an outcrop of Mount Moriah. Then he looked more carefully and he saw wood and he cleared his eyes and he saw the wood upon the back of someone moving toward this hill.

For a moment he thought that he saw Isaac, for the wood was upon him and he dragged it to the foot of the hill. Then he watched and he thought he saw them put Isaac on the wood, but then he realized that it was the Messiah. The Bible says that as he was overcome with this awful picture, he spun around and he rejoiced.

He did not weep, he did not tear his garments at the sight of an agony that is so devastating that it must tear at the human heart. The Bible says he bowed his head and he thanked God with joy. How do I know that? Because it says so in John 8:56. Listen to these words of Jesus:

> [56] "Your father Abraham rejoiced to see My day, and he saw *it* and was glad." *(John 8:56)*

"And he saw it and was glad" – is that not astonishing? "Your father Abraham rejoiced to see My day and he saw it and was glad." In other words, God gave to Abraham a birthing call in the covenant, a suffering call in the covenant, and a priestly call.

That is why it was always in the predetermined counsel and purpose of God that the Jewish people would give the death of Jesus to the world. God showed it to Abraham. And two thousand years later when the fullness of time came, Jesus came. Strange that "the fullness of time" happened to be the moment in Jewish history when the nation had passed into unbelief. They did not know God neither did they know the law or the prophets. This is the context of Jesus' incarnation.

He comes to His own and they knew Him not, so they received Him not. But like a great high priest they took Him to Moriah and they crucified Him. For the way to the city can only be through the cross.

It is not Jesus' miracles that saves you, although we thank God for them. It is not even His teaching that saves you, though we thank God for it. It is His death alone that saves you.

The Death of Jesus

The nation of Israel gave us that death. So if you ask me, "Who killed Jesus?" I will tell you, the Jews killed Jesus. Are they "Christ killers" (killers of God)? NO. Are they guilty of deicide? NO. Are they under a generational curse? NO.

Let me read for you from a few New Testament scriptures clearly stating that the Jews killed Jesus. This is the preaching of the apostolic message of the cross. This is what the early apostles preached without any type of explanation or apology.

²² "Men of Israel, hear these words: Jesus of Nazareth, a Man attested by God to you by miracles, wonders, and signs which God did through Him in your midst, as you yourselves also know— ²³ Him, being delivered by the determined purpose and foreknowledge of God, you have taken by lawless hands, have crucified, and put to death." *(Acts 2:22–23)*

³⁶ "Therefore let all the house of Israel know assuredly that God has made this Jesus, whom you crucified, both Lord and Christ."
³⁷ Now when they heard *this,* they were cut to the heart, and said to Peter and the rest of the apostles, "Men *and* brethren, what shall we do?"
(Acts 2:36-37)

¹⁴ "But you denied the Holy One and the Just, and asked for a murderer to be granted to you, ¹⁵ and killed the Prince of life, whom God raised from the dead, of which we are witnesses."
(Acts 3:14-15)

¹⁰ "let it be known to you all, and to all the people of Israel, that by the name of Jesus Christ of Nazareth, whom you crucified, whom God raised from the dead, by Him this man stands here before you whole." *(Acts 4:10)*

³⁰ "The God of our fathers raised up Jesus whom you murdered by hanging on a tree."
(Acts 5:30)

⁵¹ "*You* stiff-necked and uncircumcised in heart and ears! You always resist the Holy Spirit; as your fathers *did,* so *do* you. ⁵² Which of the

prophets did your fathers not persecute? And they killed those who foretold the coming of the Just One, of whom you now have become the betrayers and murderers." *(Acts 7:51-52)*

³⁹ "And we are witnesses of all things which He did both in the land of the Jews and in Jerusalem, whom they killed by hanging on a tree." *(Acts 10:39)*

My dear friends, I could go on. It is true the Bible says there was a conspiring between the Gentiles and the Romans for this to happen (Acts 4), but the apostolic preaching of the cross clearly states that the Jews killed Jesus.

But - big BUT - they did it in ignorance. They are not Christ killers. They are not guilty of deicide, they are not under a generational curse, for the Son of God said, "Father, forgive them, they know not what they do."

Abraham, take your son, your only begotten son, put the wood on his back. And when you get to Moriah, lay him on the wood for I am telling you, the people that come from you will have to bring the Messiah into the world and give His death to the nations.

Acts 3 is a very crucial passage in this regard. You know the story: Peter goes to the gate called Beautiful together with John, they raise up the lame man and they all gather around in Solomon's portico. Peter begins preaching in verse 13 about the God of Abraham, Isaac, and Jacob. Why? Why does he address them in that way? I will tell you why.

The God of Abraham is the God of covenant, the God of Isaac is the God of sacrifice or atonement, and the God of Jacob is the God of transformation. If God gets hold of you, you will never be the same again. Hallelujah! He is the God of Abraham, Isaac, and Jacob. He is the God of our fathers.

[13] "The God of Abraham, Isaac, and Jacob, the God of our fathers, glorified His Servant Jesus, whom you delivered up and denied in the presence of Pilate, when he was determined to let *Him* go. [14] But you denied the Holy One and the Just, and asked for a murderer to be granted to you, [15] and killed the Prince of life, whom God raised from the dead, of which we are witnesses. [16] And His name, through faith in His name, has made this man strong, whom you see and know. Yes, the faith which *comes* through Him has given him this perfect soundness in the presence of you all.
[17] Yet now, brethren, I know that you did *it* in ignorance, as *did* also your rulers."
(Acts 3:13-17)

Please underline verse 17:
[17] "Yet now, brethren, I know that you did *it* in ignorance, as *did* also your rulers."

They did it in ignorance! Do you know what the word ignorance means? It actually means ignorance! That is not difficult, is it? "Yet brethren, I know that you did it in ignorance."

In other words, they did not know what they were doing. He was not accusing them of being "Christ killers." He was not laying upon them a charge of deicide; neither was he suggesting that they and their generations are cursed and can never find their way back to God. NO! Instead, he refers then to the historical prophetic purpose of God laid upon them from the beginning.

> [17] "Yet now, brethren, I know that you did *it* in ignorance, as *did* also your rulers. [18] But those things which God foretold by the mouth of all His prophets, that the Christ would suffer, He has thus fulfilled. [19] Repent therefore and be converted, that your sins may be blotted out, so that times of refreshing may come from the presence of the Lord." *(Acts 3:17-19)*

Having said this, he offers them the gift of repentance. The Apostle Paul said the same thing in Acts 13!

> [26] "Men *and* brethren, sons of the family of Abraham, and those among you who fear God, to you the word of this salvation has been sent. [27] For those who dwell in Jerusalem, and their rulers, because they did not know Him, nor even the voices of the prophets which are read every Sabbath, have fulfilled *them* in condemning *Him.*" *(Acts 13:26-27)*

They did not know Him. They had drifted so far from their own scriptures that when He came, they rejected Him. Yet in that rejection, and in that inability to discern Him, they fulfilled the very thing that God wanted from them, the death of Jesus.

In Acts 3, Peter linked the death of Jesus to the Abrahamic covenant.

[24] "Yes, and all the prophets, from Samuel and those who follow, as many as have spoken, have also foretold these days. [25]You are sons of the prophets, and of the covenant which God made with our fathers, saying to Abraham, 'And in your seed all the families of the earth shall be blessed.' [26]To you first, God, having raised up His Servant Jesus, sent Him to bless you, in turning away every one of you from your iniquities."   *(Acts 3:24-26)*

How will the families of the earth come home? How will they be blessed? Only by the cross. There is no other way.

Israel's Return Home

The Bible teaches us that there will be two exiles and two returns of the Jewish people in history. Isaiah 11:11 teaches this very clearly.

> It shall come to pass in that day
> *That* the Lord shall set His hand again the second time
> To recover the remnant of His people who are left,
> From Assyria and Egypt,
> From Pathros and Cush,
> From Elam and Shinar,
> From Hamath and the islands of the sea.
> *(Isaiah 11:11)*

Then will He gather for "the *second* time." The first exile of Israel took place in 586 B.C. and the second exile took place in 70 A.D. They have now returned for the second and last time to the land that God promised to Abraham as an everlasting possession.

The Bible further tells us from the prophets that the latter day and final day of return of the Jewish people to the land of Canaan will have two phases. It will have a physical phase, to be followed by a spiritual phase. That is, they will come home a secular or unbelieving people, and then there will be an outpouring of God's love and Spirit upon them and they will be spiritually recovered.

> [24] "For I will take you from among the nations, gather you out of all countries, and bring you into your own land. [25] Then I will sprinkle clean water on you, and you shall be clean; I will cleanse you from all your filthiness and from all your idols. [26] I will give you a new heart and put a new spirit within you; I will take the heart of stone out of your flesh and give you a heart of flesh. [27] I will put My Spirit within you and cause you to walk in My statutes, and you will keep My judgments and do them. [28] Then you shall dwell in the land that I gave to your fathers; you shall be My people, and I will be your God." *(Ezekiel 36:24-28)*

Here the Word of God teaches there is coming a day when Israel will return in unbelief to the land of her forefathers. Her physical return will be followed by a spiritual recovery. And this, according to Ezekiel, because of the promise God gave to her fathers. Which fathers? To Abraham, Isaac, and Jacob. In other words, Israel's last restoration takes place because of the Abrahamic covenant.

My dear friends, the Jewish people have returned home for the last time. I have to tell you that the conflict of all history is upon us because God's birthing people have come home. The "woman" is home again, and we have moved into the final act of human history. The events which are unfolding in the Middle East tonight will find their culmination with the return of the "male Child."

Basis of Christian Support for Israel

Israel is God's birthing people. She birthed Him into the world the first time and she has gone back to birth Him into the world a second time. When the Messiah comes, the Bible teaches us, all demonic influence all over the world will come to an end (Revelation 20:1-3).

You can therefore appreciate, if the "vulture" has resisted this people for 4,000 years, that he will now resist this people more than any other nation group upon the face of the earth, because in their physical and spiritual recovery is the demise of demonic influence and power over the world.

Israel will bring the King home and He will put His feet upon the Mount of Olives and He will reign from shore to shore and the nations will not learn war anymore. He will rule them with a rod of iron because He is the Lion of the Tribe of Judah. His name is Jesus!

Many think that the Middle East conflict is a secular political conflict. It is not. It has everything to do with the final purpose of God for the redemption of the world.

That is why Revelation 16:13-16 says that unclean spirits like frogs go out of the mouth of the dragon to the four corners of the earth. This is the same fiery dragon that stood before the pregnant woman in Revelation 12. The three unclean spirits like frogs go out of the mouth of this dragon and they go to the four corners of the earth to seduce the kings and politicians of the world. To do what? To come up in battle against tiny Israel. The vulture is on the move!

The book of Revelation states that nation after nation will be seduced by the speaking of these unclean spirits. The media distortions concerning the conflict in Israel have made this a global reality of our times. How else could it be that 59% of Europeans believe that Israel is the greatest threat to world peace? The answer can only be that the lies of the demonic frogs have been bought and broadcast by the world's media.

Now we go in conclusion to Acts 3. The Apostle Peter understood something, and this is what it is.

[17] "Yet now, brethren, I know that you did *it* in ignorance, as *did* also your rulers. [18] But those things which God foretold by the mouth of all His prophets, that the Christ would suffer, He has thus fulfilled. [19] Repent therefore and be converted, that your sins may be blotted out, so that times of refreshing may come from the presence of the Lord." *(Acts 3:17-19)*

Those things which God foretold by the mouth of all His prophets that the Christ would suffer, He has thus fulfilled. What should Israel do and what will happen when Israel does it?

This is not Plan B, this is Plan A. He says when Israel is spiritually recovered, this recovery will be the trigger mechanism for the return of Jesus.

[19] "Repent therefore and be converted, that your sins may be blotted out, so that times of refreshing may come from the presence of the Lord, [20] and that He may send Jesus Christ, who was preached to you before, [21] whom heaven must receive [Greek: keep or retain] until the

times of restoration of all things, which God has spoken by the mouth of all His holy prophets since the world began." *(Acts 3:19-21)*

In the final analysis, this conflict in the Middle East, dear friends, is about the redemption of Israel. It is about the throne of the Lord in Zion. It is all about the male Child who is destined to rule the nations with a rod of iron. My dear friends, this is the basis of Biblical Zionism and of our support of Israel.

Your Embassy in Jerusalem

The International Christian Embassy Jerusalem was established in 1980 in recognition of the biblical significance of Jerusalem and its unique connection to the Jewish people. Today, it represents millions of Christians, churches, and denominations to the nation and people. We recognize that the restoration of the State of Israel reflects God's faithfulness in keeping His ancient covenant with the Jewish people.

Our main objectives are to stand with Israel in support and friendship, equip and teach the worldwide church regarding God's purposes with Israel, and be a reconciling influence between Jews, Christians, and Arabs. Our work with its head office in Jerusalem reaches more than 140 countries with branch offices in over 80 nations.

SUPPORTING ISRAEL

AID PROJECTS: For over 35 years the ICEJ has been building relationships, fostering reconciliation and sharing God's love in Israel through a wide variety of humanitarian projects that respond to many areas of pressing social need. From providing emergency relief to victims of terror to caring for elderly Holocaust survivors, ICEJ AID projects have touched almost every community and people group in the land.

ADVOCACY: Through our network of national directors and representatives across the globe, we raise support for the people of Israel through solidarity rallies, teaching events, and advocacy campaigns. We engage with pastors, governments, and local Jewish communities, recognizing our scriptural responsibility to stand with the Jewish people, while also promoting Christian tourism and an understanding of Israel.

ALIYAH: In the 1980s the ICEJ was at the forefront of worldwide efforts to support the persecuted Soviet Jews. Since then we have helped more than 120,000 Jews return "home" to Israel and offered practical support to assist thousands more upon arrival in the land. Recent Aliyah initiatives have focused on the last remaining Ethiopian Jews, the lost tribe of Manasseh (Bnei Menashe from India), French Jews, and Ukrainian Jews.

PROMOTING JUSTICE

ANTI-SEMITISM: The ICEJ is called to confront the rising tide of hostility that threatens the nation of Israel and Jewish community worldwide. In late 2006 we forged an historic partnership with Yad Vashem, Israel's Holocaust Remembrance Center, aimed at helping Christians better understand the roots of the Nazi Holocaust and be mobilized to confront modern anti-Semitism in all its forms. Christian Friends of Yad Vashem represents a major breakthrough in Jewish-Christian relations at a time when Islamic leaders are stepping up their efforts to demonize Israel and threatening another genocide against the Jewish people. In addition to these church-wide educational efforts, the ICEJ is ministering in practical ways to the aging generation of Holocaust survivors in Israel, having established the nation's first dedicated assisted-living home for them in Haifa.

PERSECUTION: Islamic extremism is not just a threat to Israel, but is responsible for the persecution of Christians and oppression of women throughout the Middle East. So, in addition to efforts to assist our beleaguered brethren in the Palestinian areas, and Christian Syrian and Iraqi refugees fleeing civil war and ethnic cleansing, we have offered support to hundreds of African refugees who have fled Muslim warlords in Sudan and persecution in Egypt.

TEACHING TRUTH

AT THE FEAST: The ICEJ is probably best known for hosting the Christian celebration of the Feast of Tabernacles—a multicultural event that draws thousands of pilgrims to Jerusalem from over 80 nations for teaching, worship, and prayer. As the largest annual tourist event in Israel, the Feast has a tremendous economic and spiritual impact on ordinary Israelis, and also points to the day when all the earth will worship the one, true God in Zion.

TO THE NATIONS: Reaching out in many languages through television, print, and electronic media, the ICEJ educates Christians all over the world about Israel's unique calling, political situation, and social challenges. Embassy speakers and educational seminars have brought the prophetic message of Israel's restoration to churches across the US, Europe, South America, Africa, India, Asia, and beyond.

ACROSS GENERATIONS: Arise, the ICEJ Young Adults program, seeks to raise up a new generation of Christian leaders who will grasp God's covenant purposes for the nation of Israel and take up the challenge to stand with the Jewish people in these days. Arise ministers to youth groups and churches in the nations and hosts short-term tours to Israel while offering a unique blend of study and service opportunities for young adults ages 18-30.

ICEJ BIBLICAL ZIONISM SERIES

The Basis of Christian Support for Israel
The basis of Christian support for Israel is found in God's promises to Abraham. The Abrahamic covenant declared God's love for the world and his establishment of a people through which to redeem the world. Israel's unique calling is still in force today and her return home to the land given to Abraham is evidence of that. ISBN# 978-0-9765297-0-5

The Heart of Biblical Zionism
Clear biblical principles concerning God's dealings with Israel and the nations are the framework for an accurate interpretation of God's promises and calling on national Israel. Biblical Zionism is clearly defined and put in the correct theological context in this teaching.
ISBN# 978-0-9765297-1-2

The Great Covenants of the Bible
This exciting study of the four great covenants of the Bible also refutes Replacement Theology which teaches that the church has replaced Israel and Israel no longer has a unique call or destiny.
ISBN# 978-0-9765297-2-9

The New Testament and Israel
The New Testament validates a number of Old Testament doctrines concerning Israel. Foremost it affirms that God has not gone back on His promises to Israel.
ISBN# 978-0-9765297-3-6

The Celebration of the Feast of Tabernacles
The Feast of Tabernacles is a celebration of the triumph of the kingdom of God and as such is now celebrated annually by Christians around the world.
ISBN# 978-0-9765297-4-3

BIBLICAL ZIONISM STUDY

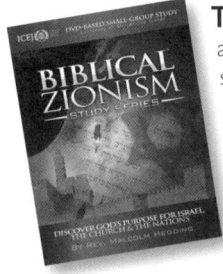

The Biblical Zionism Study Series is almost 8 hours of in-depth teaching, formatted for small group study, on the basis of Biblical Zionism. It provides foundational teaching truths dealing with the calling of Abraham, the land of Israel, the great covenants of the Bible, and replacement theology. While watching the teachings on DVD, students complete a fill-in-the-blank listening guide then participate in group discussion.

ICEJ PUBLICATIONS

The ICEJ is committed to educating the Church worldwide about Israel, and about current events in the Middle East.

Sign up for our various publications including the ICEJ *Word from Jerusalem* magazine, or sign up for additional news, commentary and teaching resources from Israel.

**Sign up today at: www.icejusa.org/icej-publications
or by calling (615) 895-9830**

P.O. Box 332974 • Murfreesboro, TN 37133 • www.icejusa.org